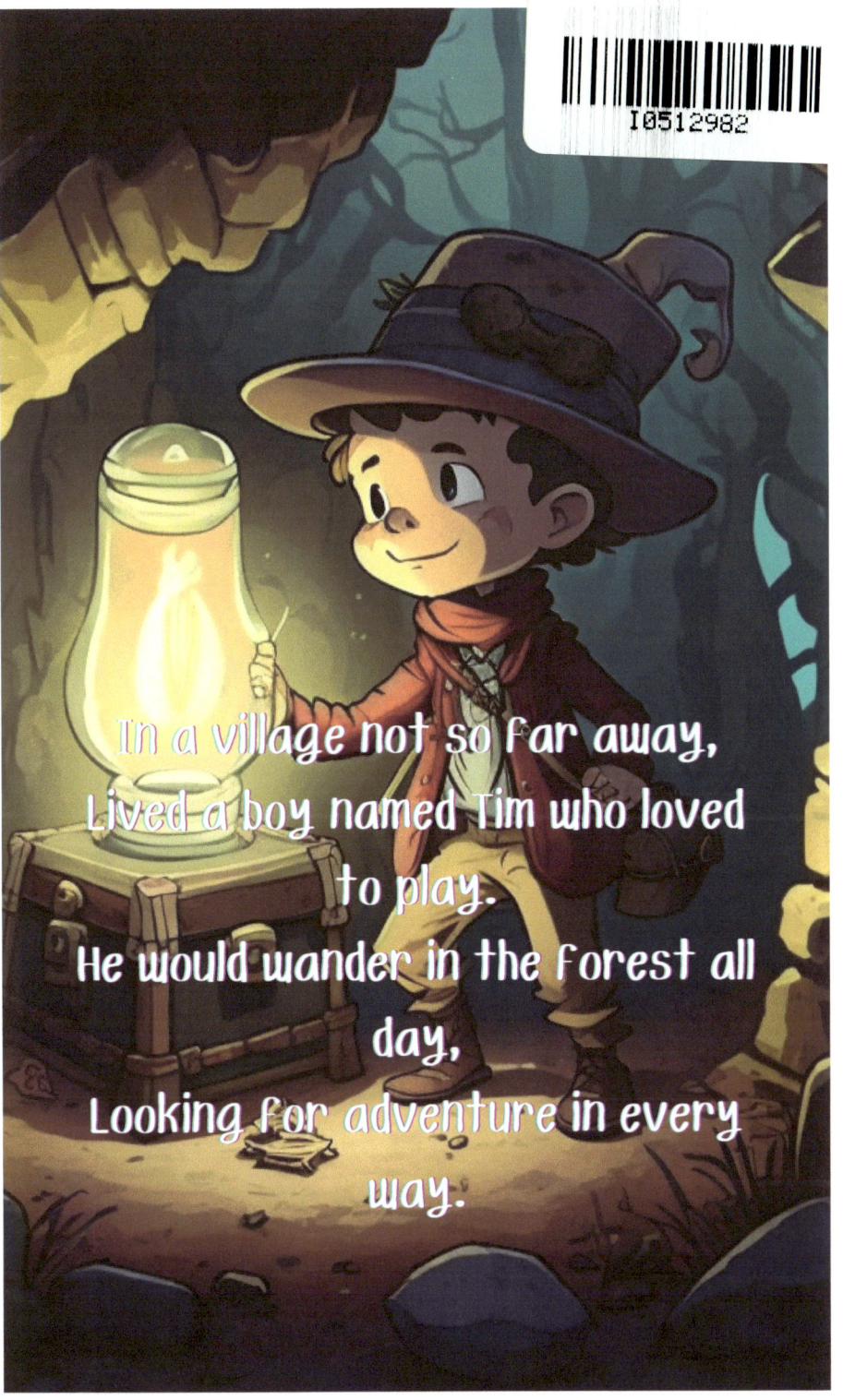

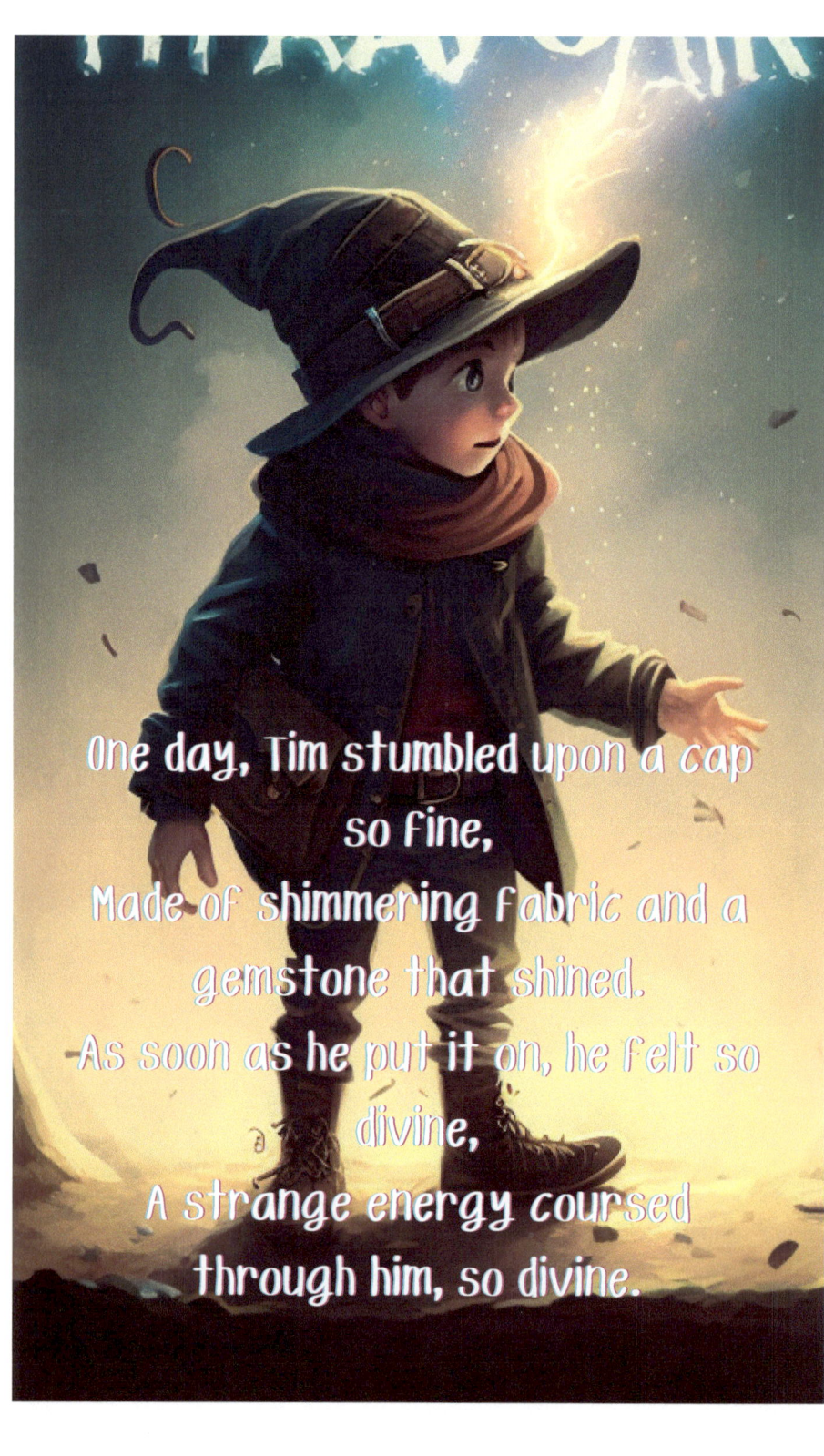

One day, Tim stumbled upon a cap so fine,
Made of shimmering fabric and a gemstone that shined.
As soon as he put it on, he felt so divine,
A strange energy coursed through him, so divine.

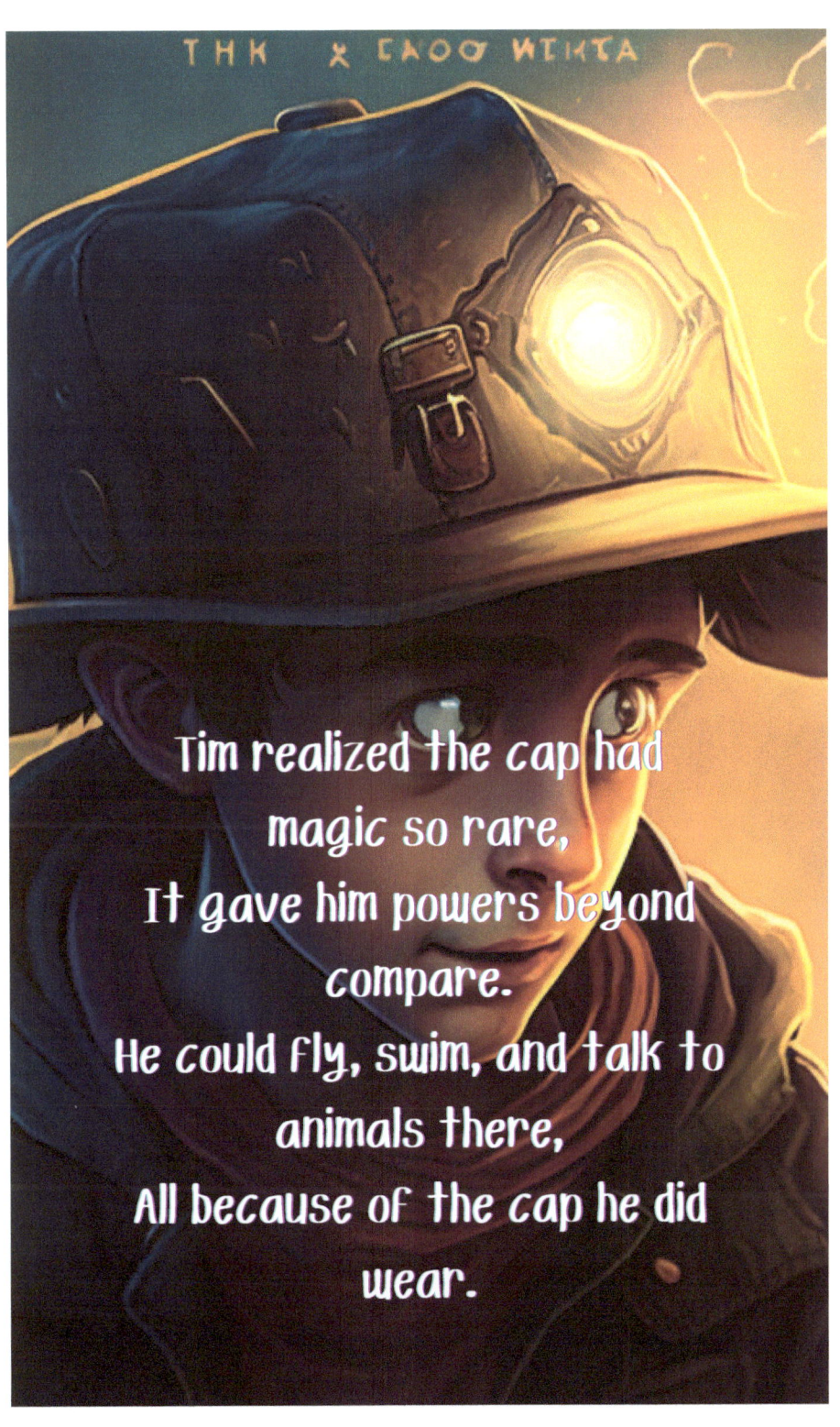

Tim realized the cap had magic so rare,
It gave him powers beyond compare.
He could fly, swim, and talk to animals there,
All because of the cap he did wear.

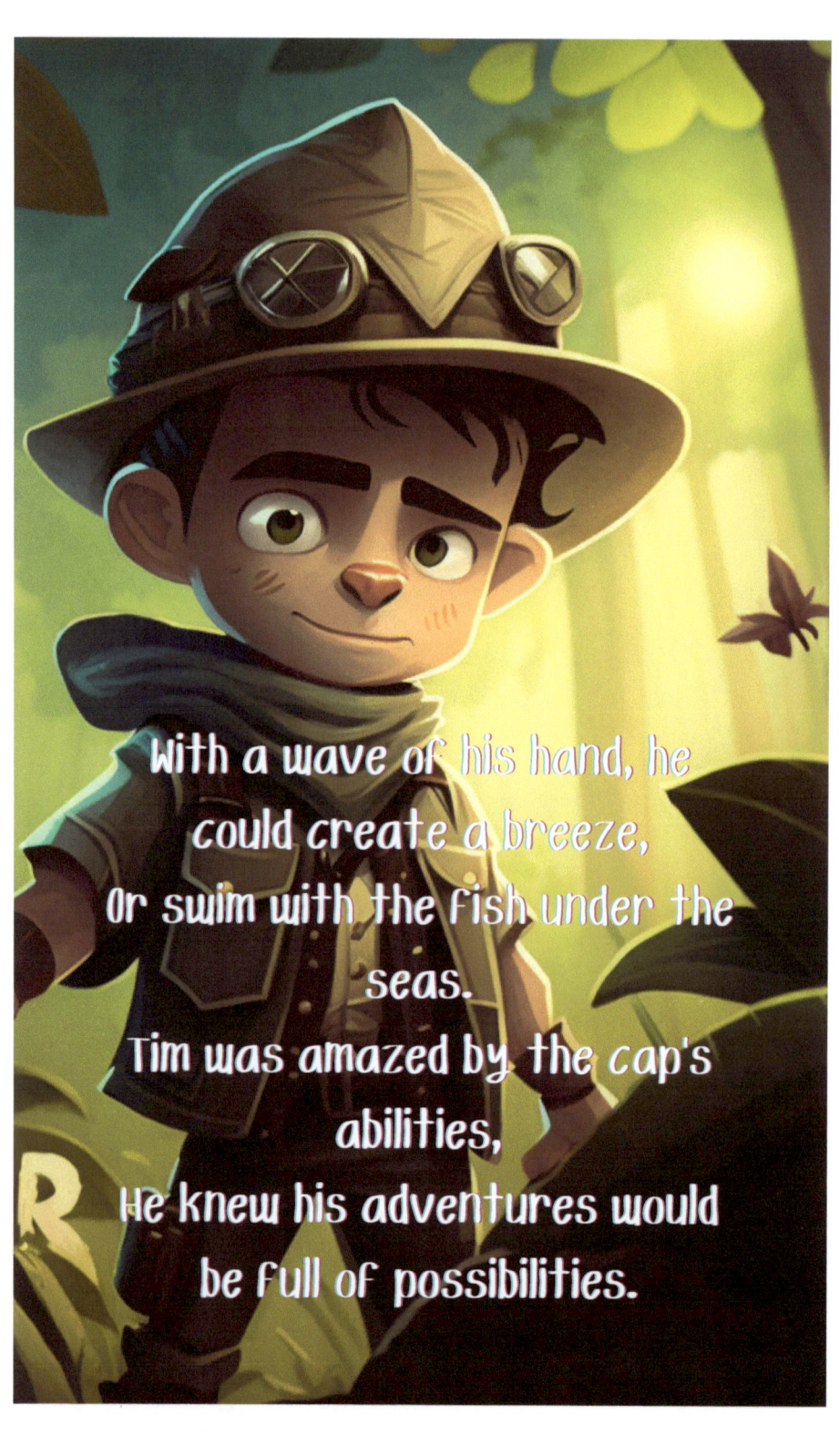

With a wave of his hand, he could create a breeze,
Or swim with the fish under the seas.
Tim was amazed by the cap's abilities,
He knew his adventures would be full of possibilities.

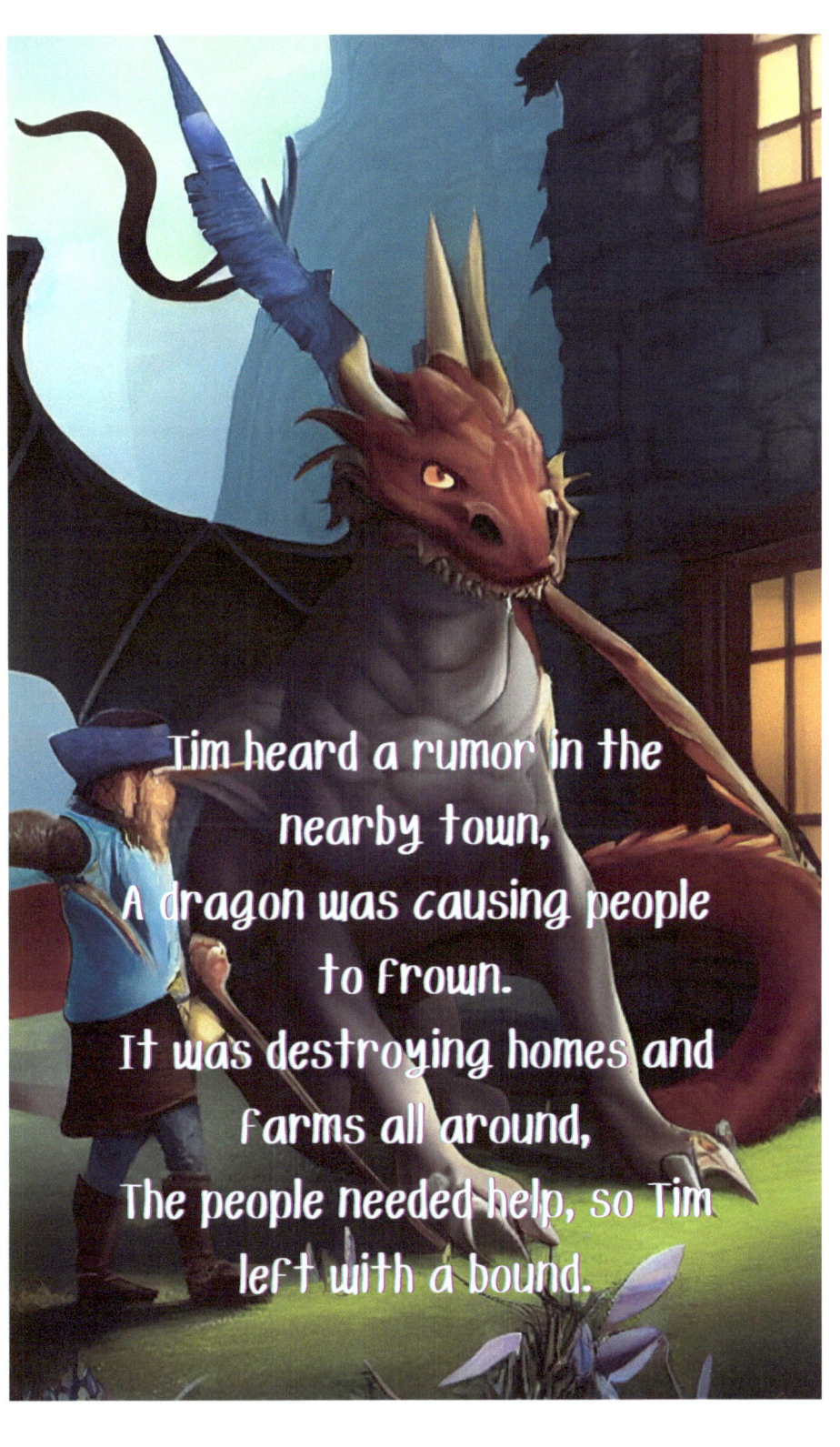

Tim heard a rumor in the nearby town,
A dragon was causing people to frown.
It was destroying homes and farms all around,
The people needed help, so Tim left with a bound.

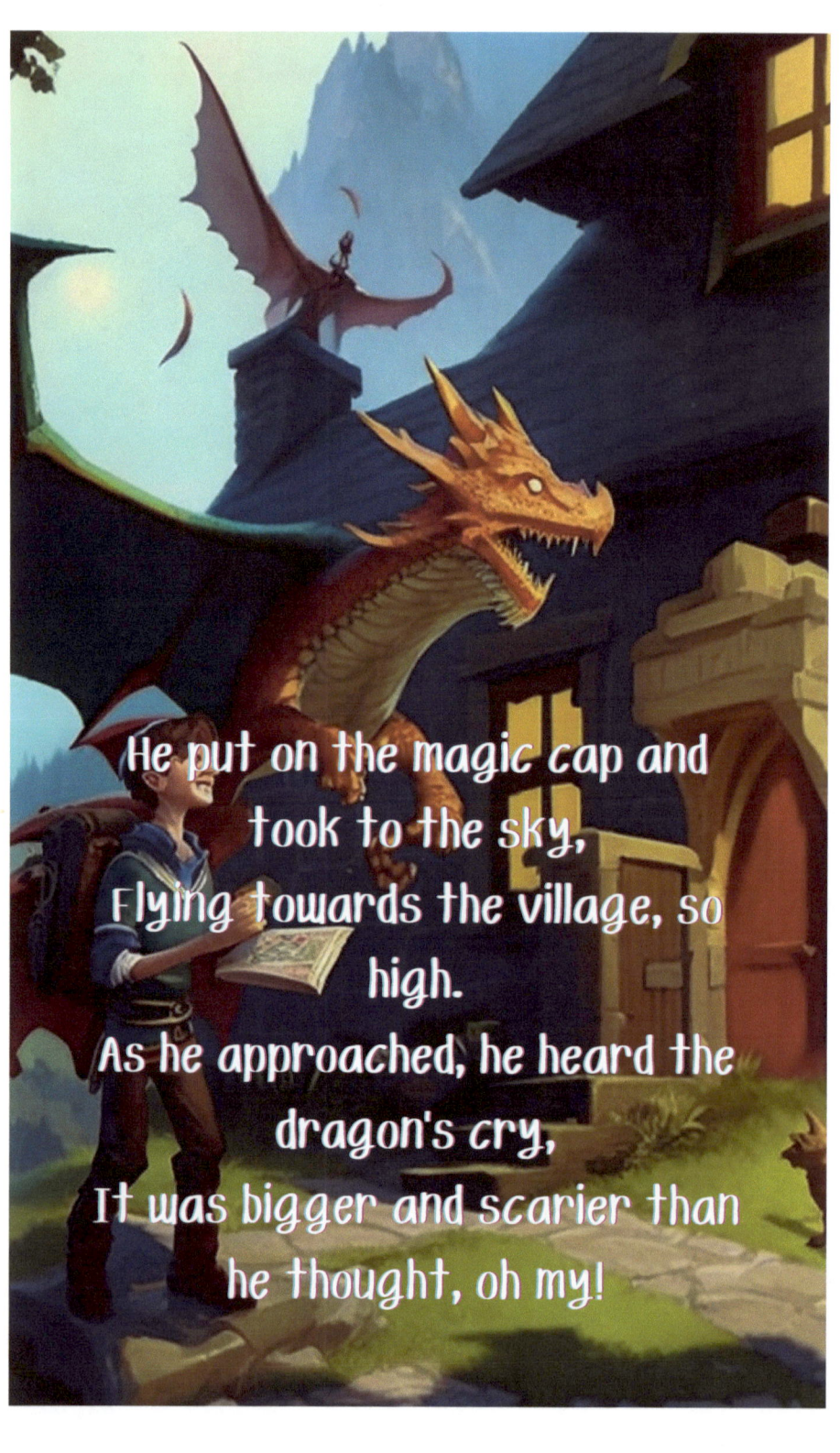

He put on the magic cap and took to the sky,
Flying towards the village, so high.
As he approached, he heard the dragon's cry,
It was bigger and scarier than he thought, oh my!

With a deep breath, Tim descended to the ground,
Ready to defeat the dragon, he was resound.
He used his powers to make a loud sound,
The dragon was startled and turned around.

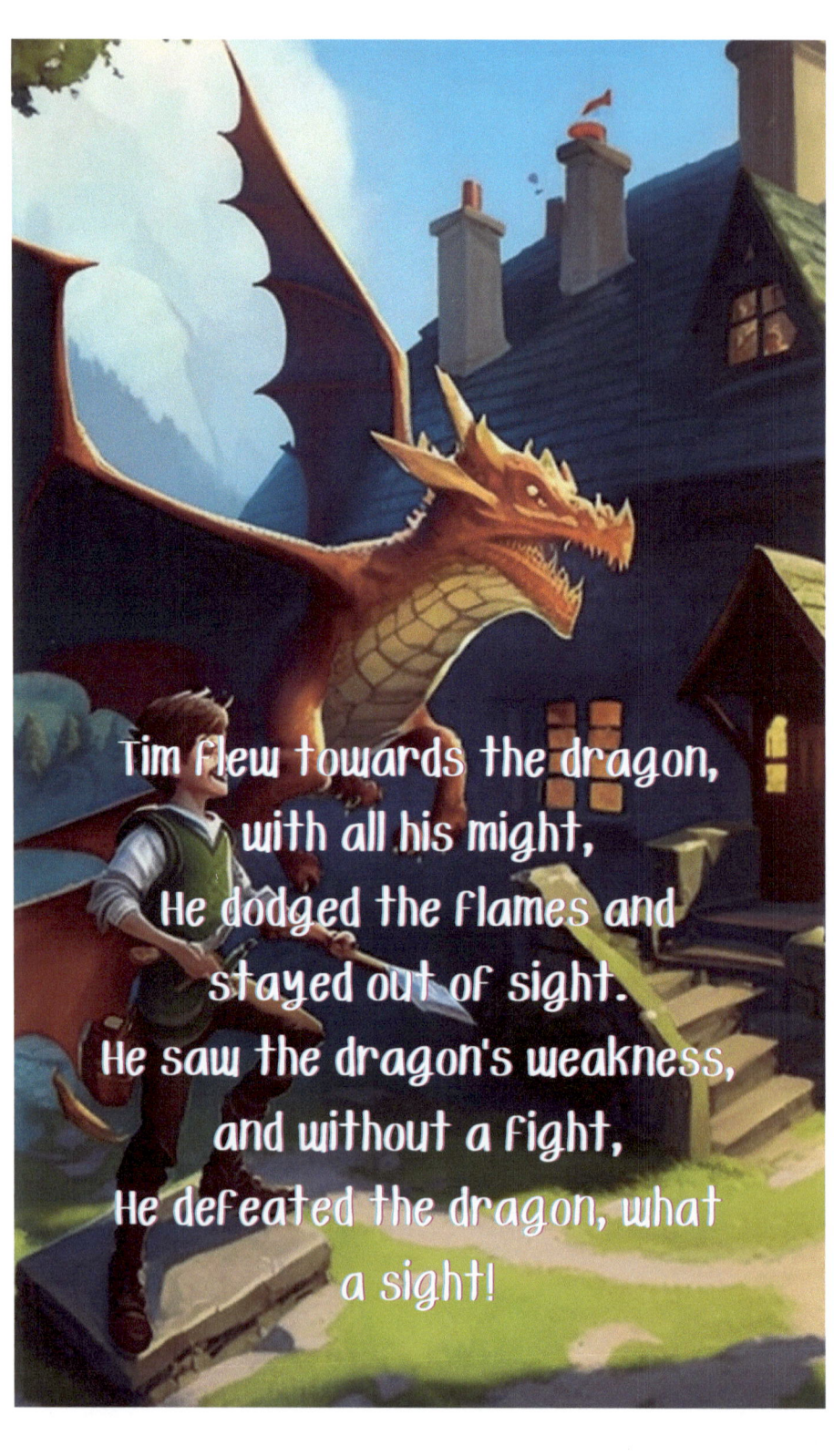

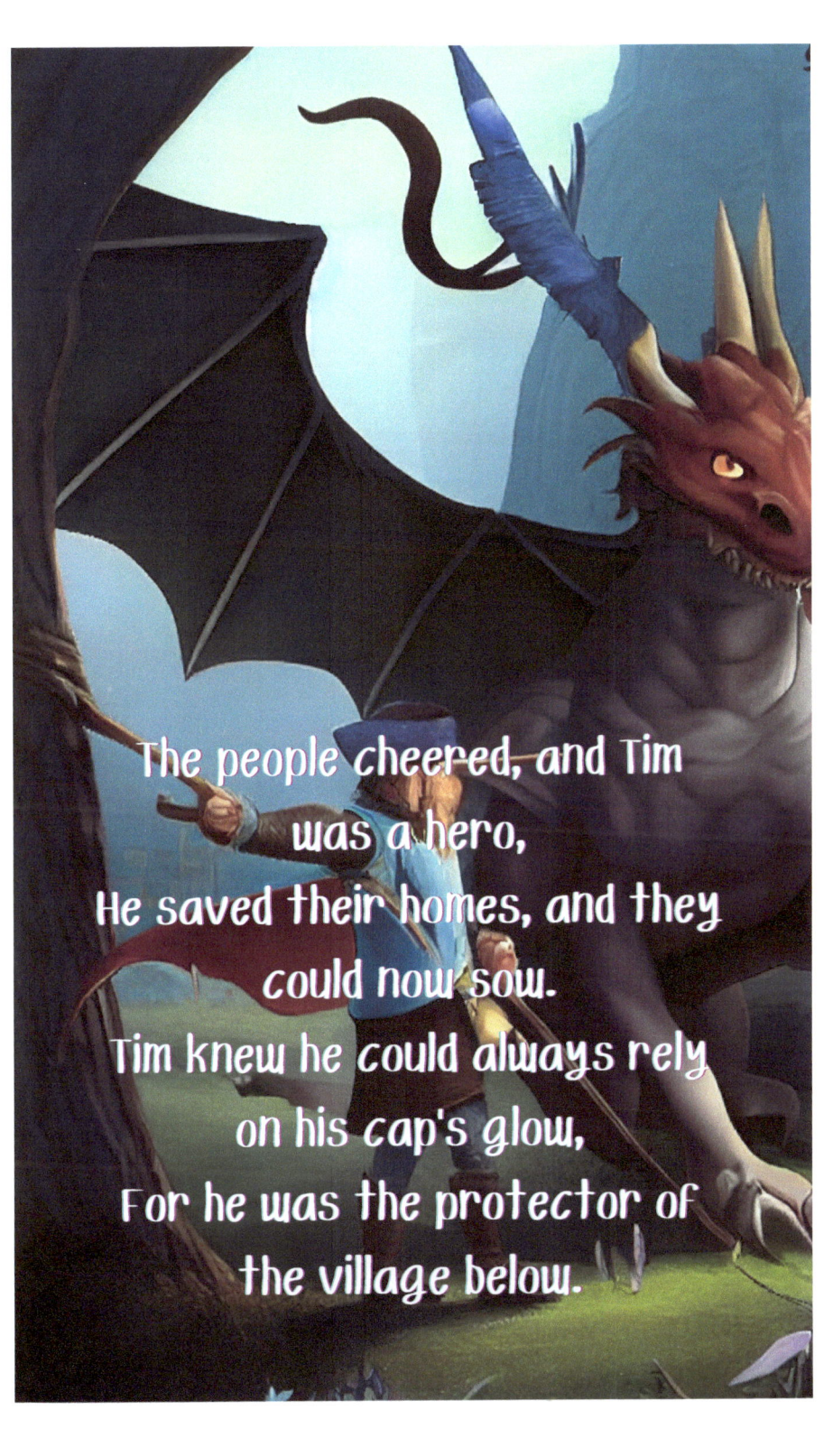

The people cheered, and Tim
was a hero,
He saved their homes, and they
could now sow.
Tim knew he could always rely
on his cap's glow,
For he was the protector of
the village below.

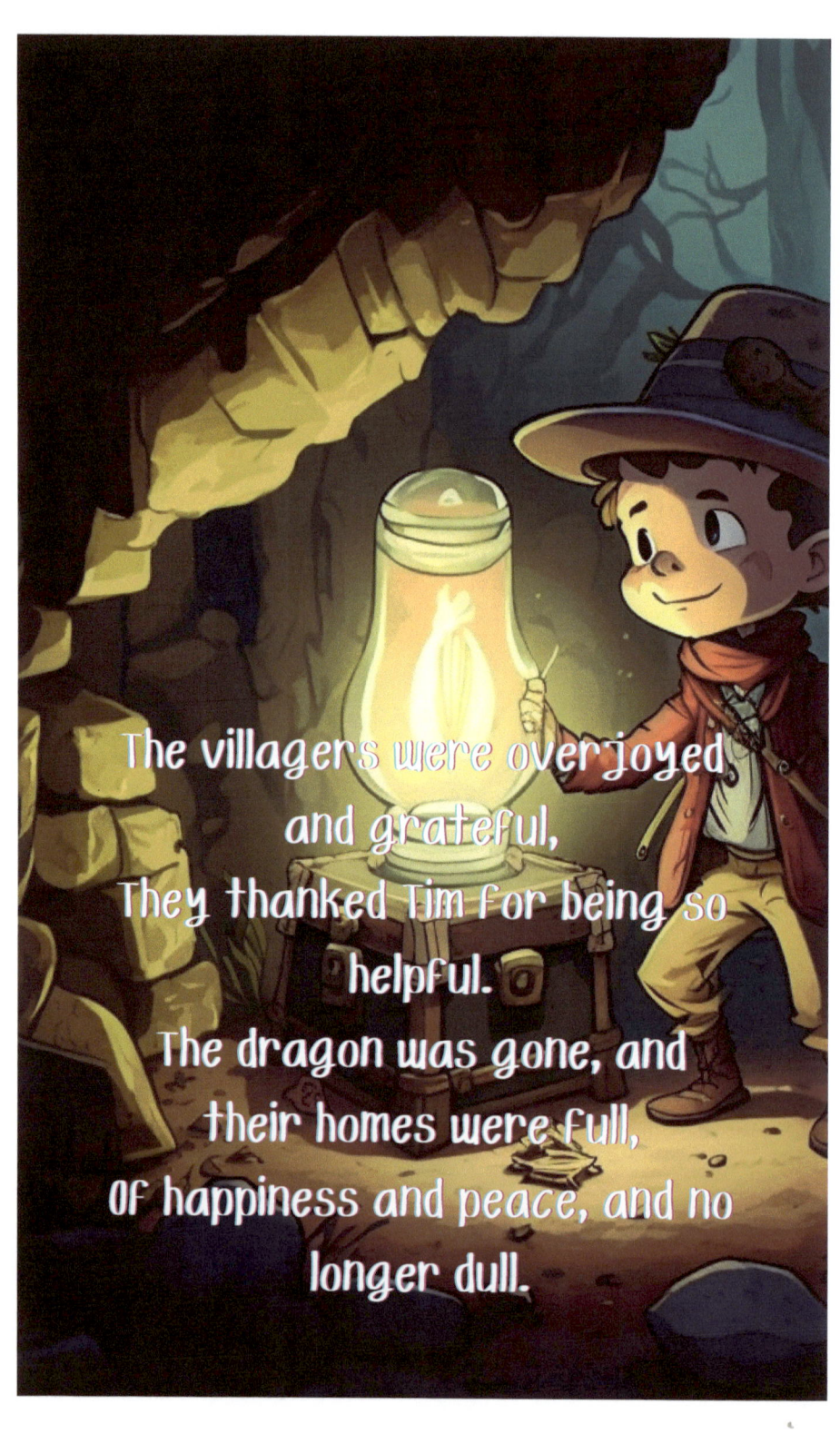

Tim became known as the village protector,
A hero who never failed to garner respect, sir.
He was always ready to offer help and sector,
Using his magic cap as the key connector.

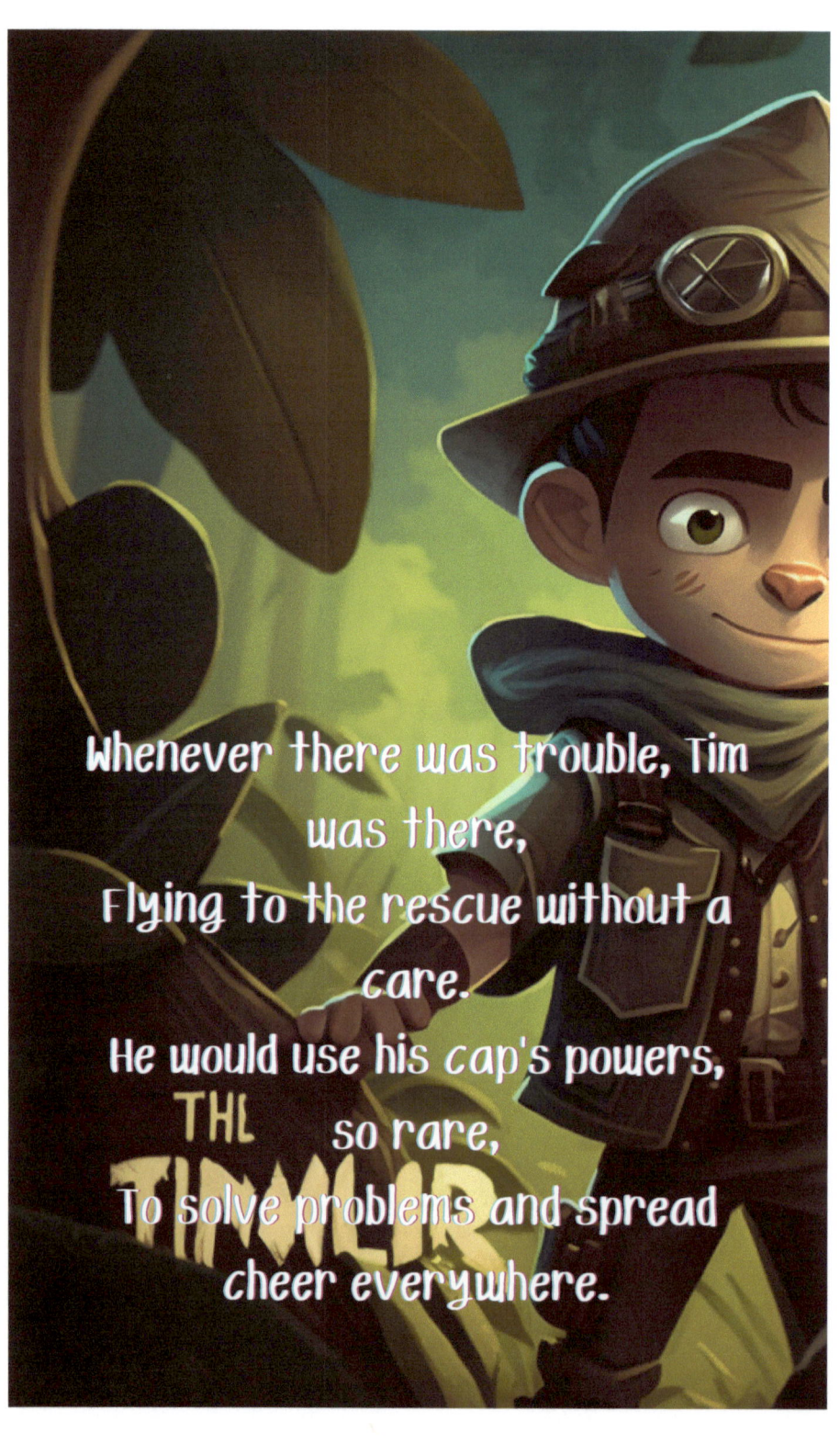

Whenever there was trouble, Tim was there,
Flying to the rescue without a care.
He would use his cap's powers, so rare,
To solve problems and spread cheer everywhere.

The villagers knew they could
always count on Tim,
For he was brave, kind, and
always full of vim.
He continued to use his magic cap
to the brim,
Helping others and making the
world a little less grim.

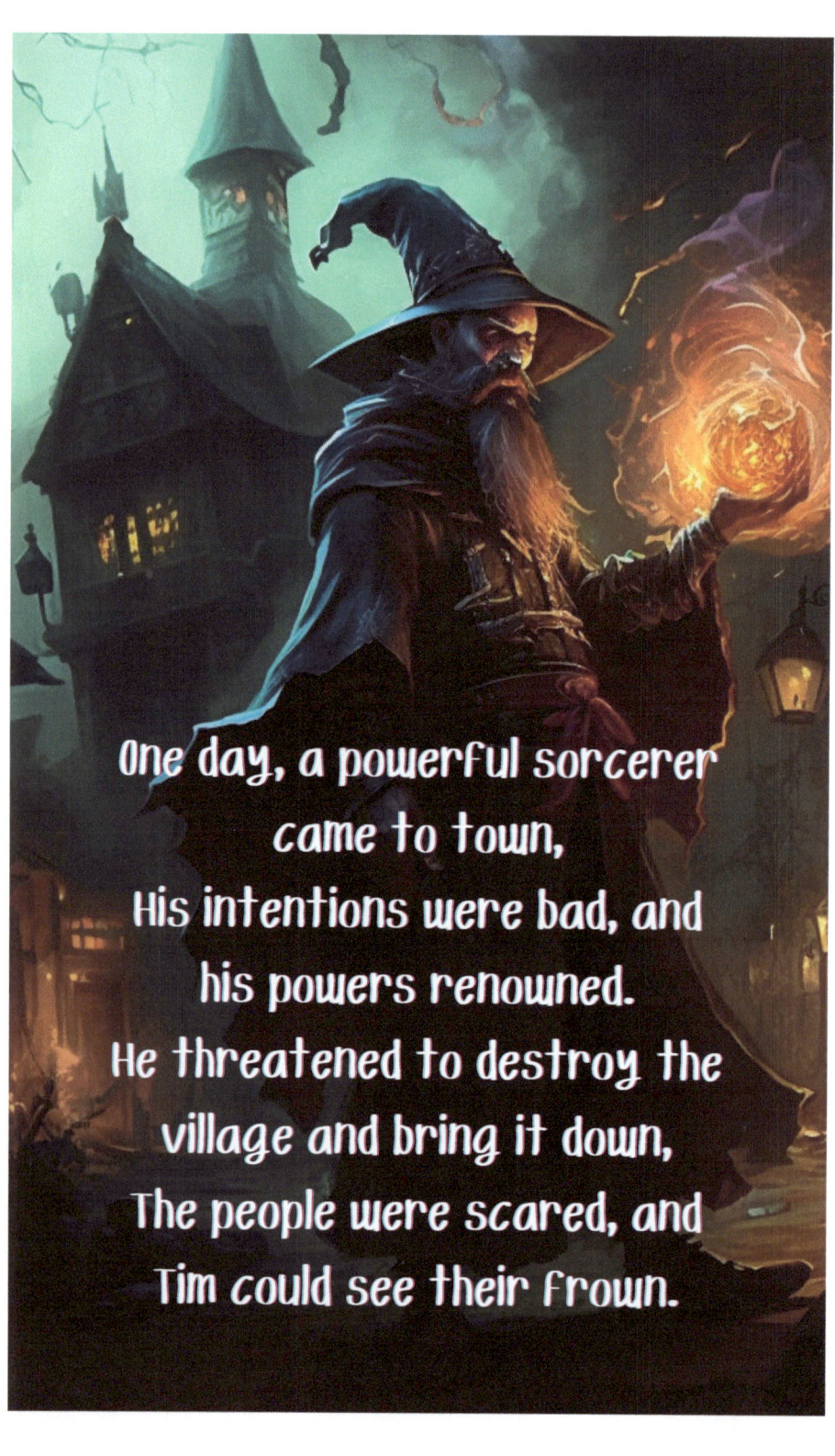

One day, a powerful sorcerer
came to town,
His intentions were bad, and
his powers renowned.
He threatened to destroy the
village and bring it down,
The people were scared, and
Tim could see their frown.

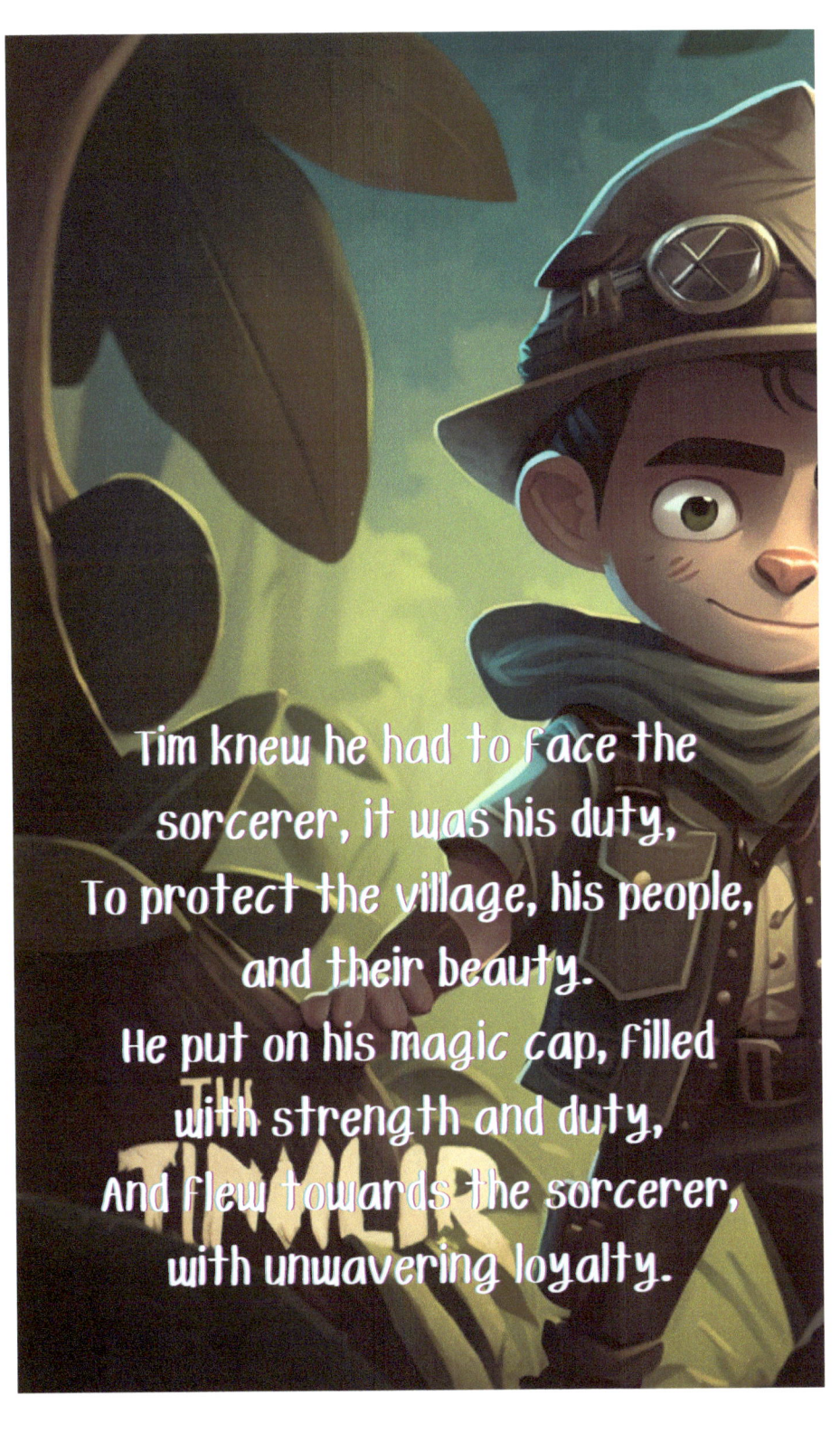

Tim knew he had to face the sorcerer, it was his duty,
To protect the village, his people, and their beauty.
He put on his magic cap, filled with strength and duty,
And flew towards the sorcerer, with unwavering loyalty.

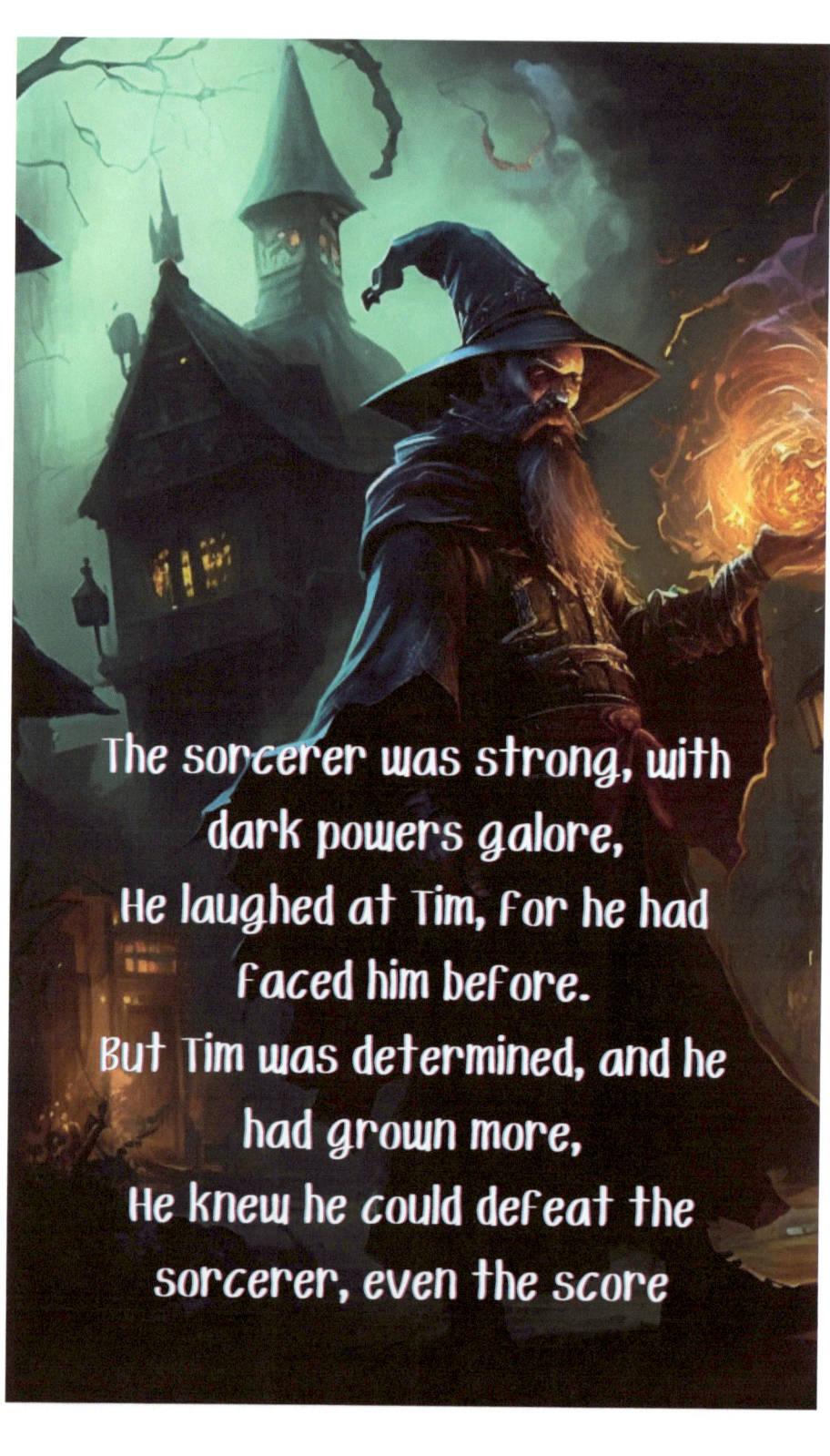

The sorcerer was strong, with
dark powers galore,
He laughed at Tim, for he had
faced him before.
But Tim was determined, and he
had grown more,
He knew he could defeat the
sorcerer, even the score

With a wave of his hand, Tim created a shield,
To protect himself from the sorcerer's sword and yield.
He used all his powers and never once kneeled,
Until the sorcerer was defeated, and the village was healed.

The people cheered, and Tim was a true hero,
For he had saved their village from destruction and zero.
He had faced his fears and shown great bravado,
Using his magic cap and heart's motto.

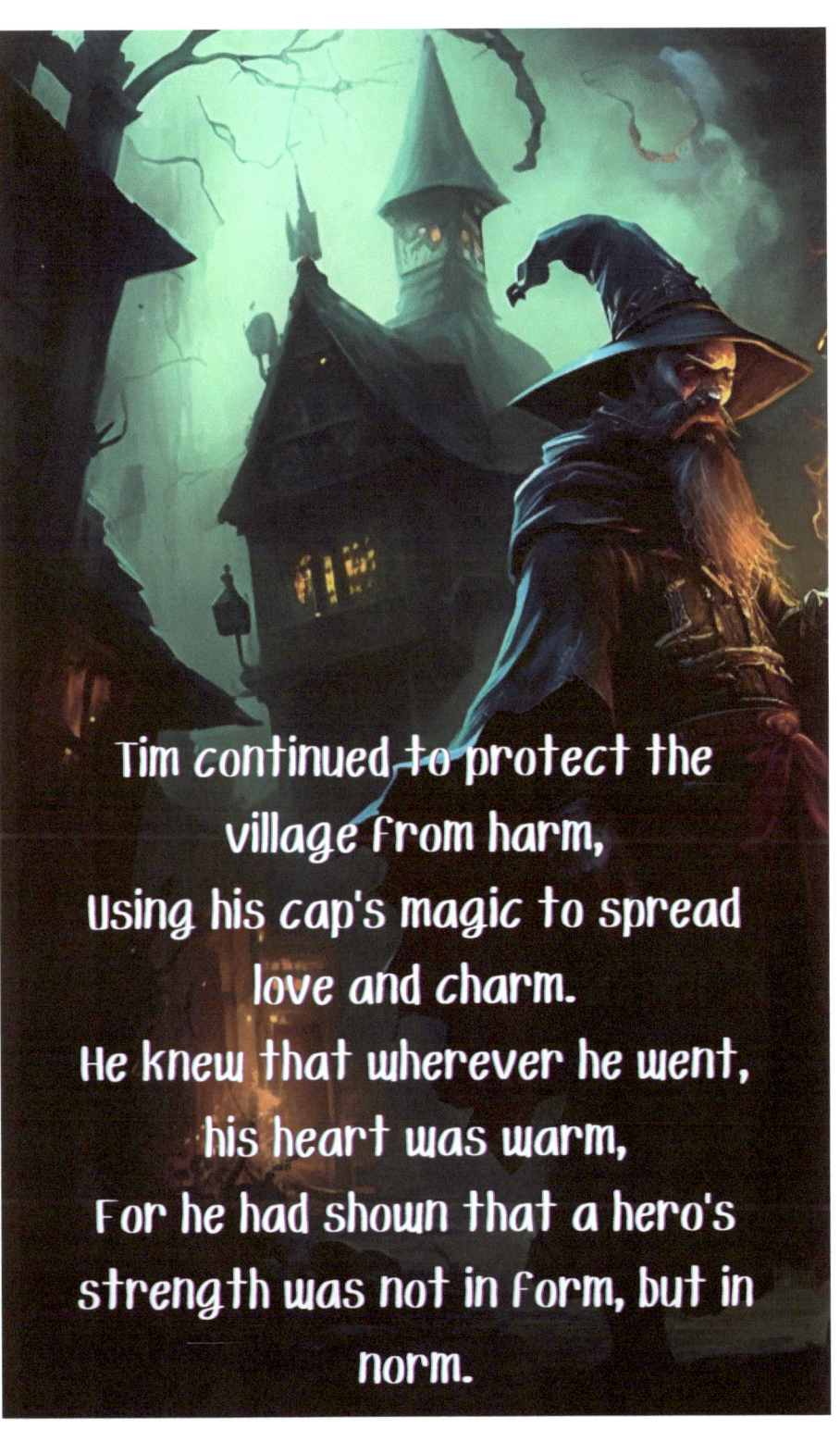

Tim continued to protect the village from harm,
Using his cap's magic to spread love and charm.
He knew that wherever he went, his heart was warm,
For he had shown that a hero's strength was not in form, but in norm.

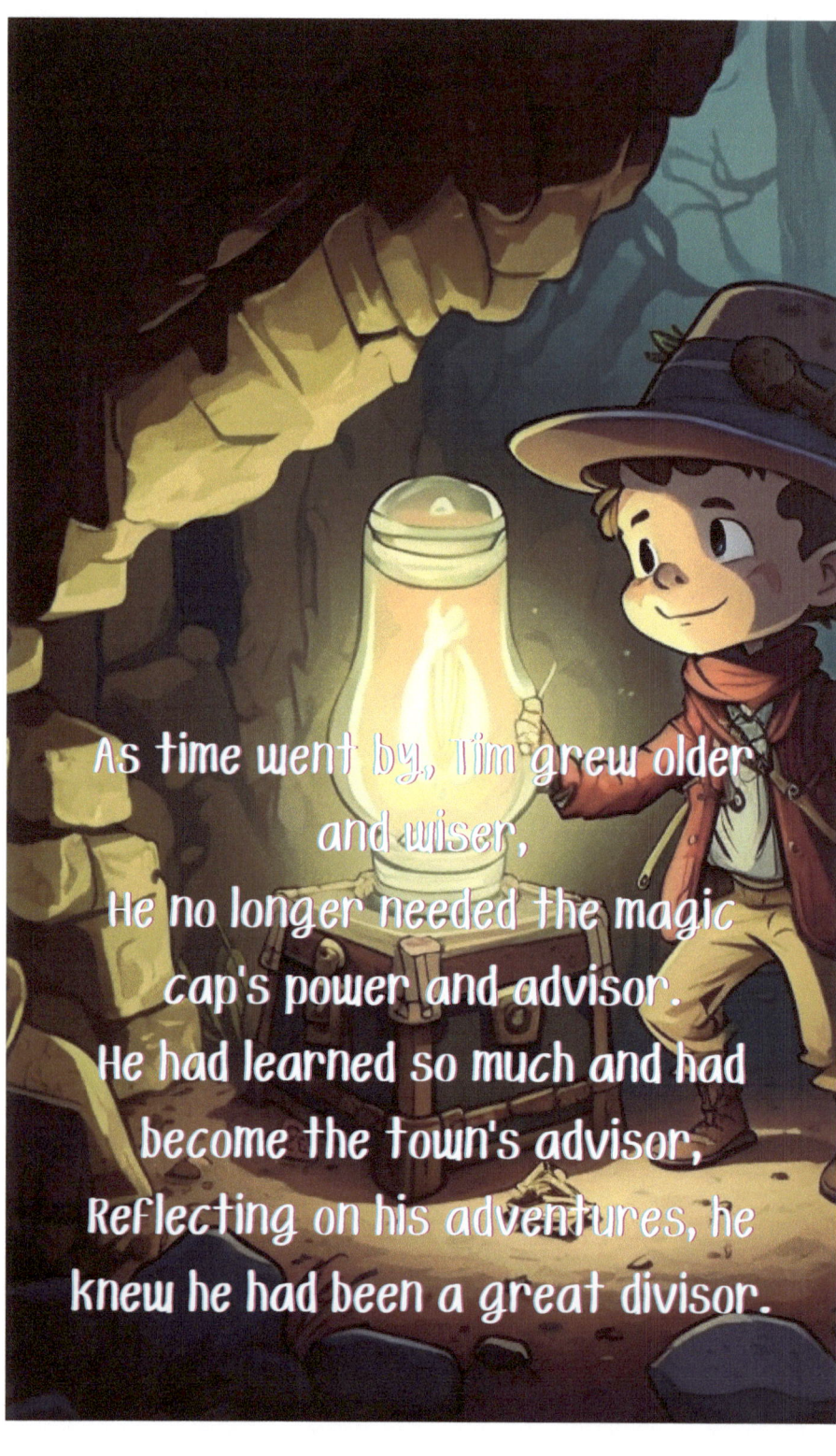

As time went by, Tim grew older and wiser,
He no longer needed the magic cap's power and advisor.
He had learned so much and had become the town's advisor,
Reflecting on his adventures, he knew he had been a great divisor.

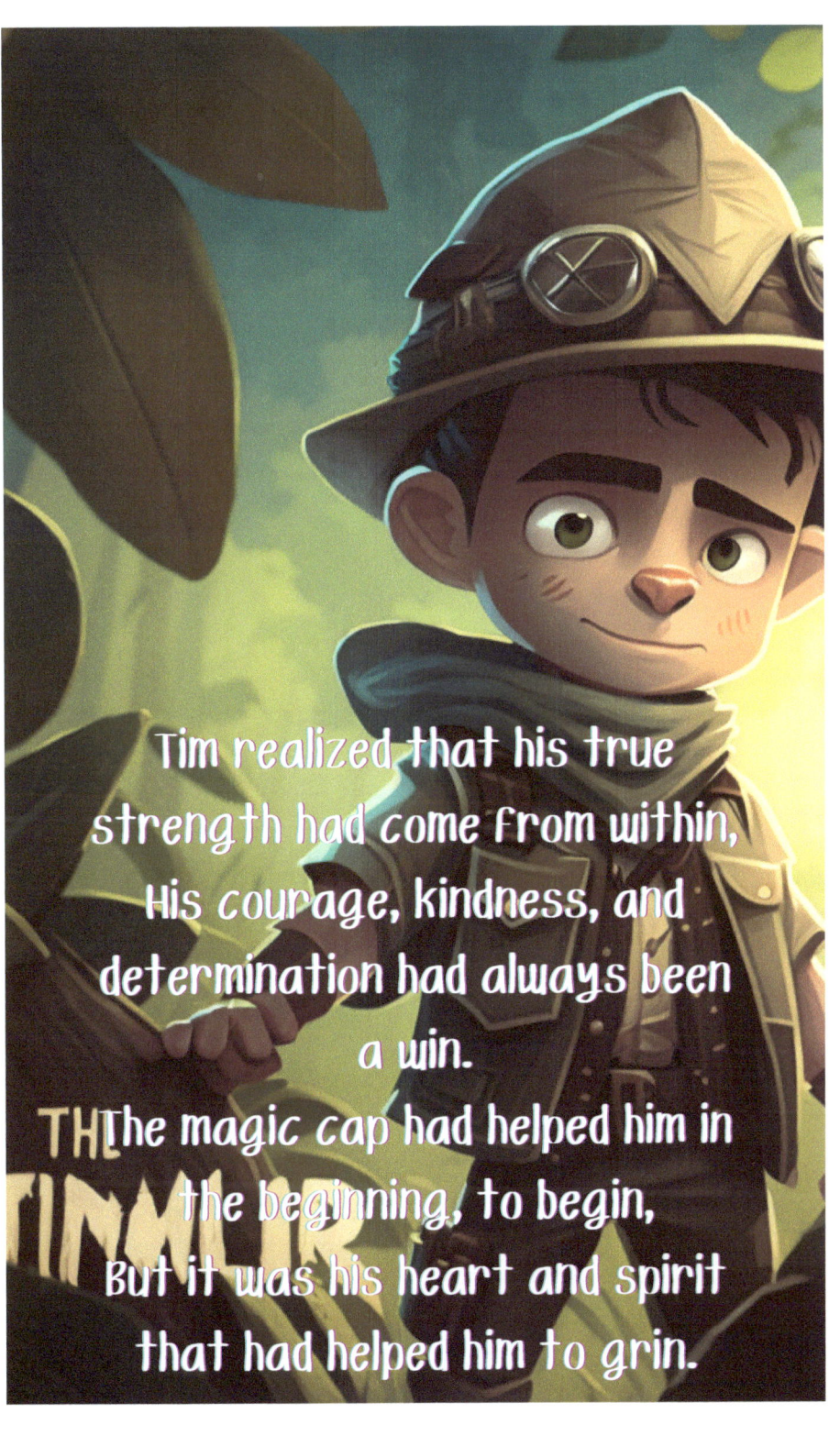

Tim realized that his true strength had come from within,
His courage, kindness, and determination had always been a win.
The magic cap had helped him in the beginning, to begin,
But it was his heart and spirit that had helped him to grin.

He thought about all the people
he had helped,
From the dragon to the
sorcerer, he had never yelped.
The villagers had always looked
up to him and had never kelped,
For he was their hero, a shining
example that had never whelped.

Tim knew that he would always
be remembered,
As the hero who had never
surrendered.
He had shown that kindness and
courage were never rendered,
And that with a strong heart,
anything could be tendered.

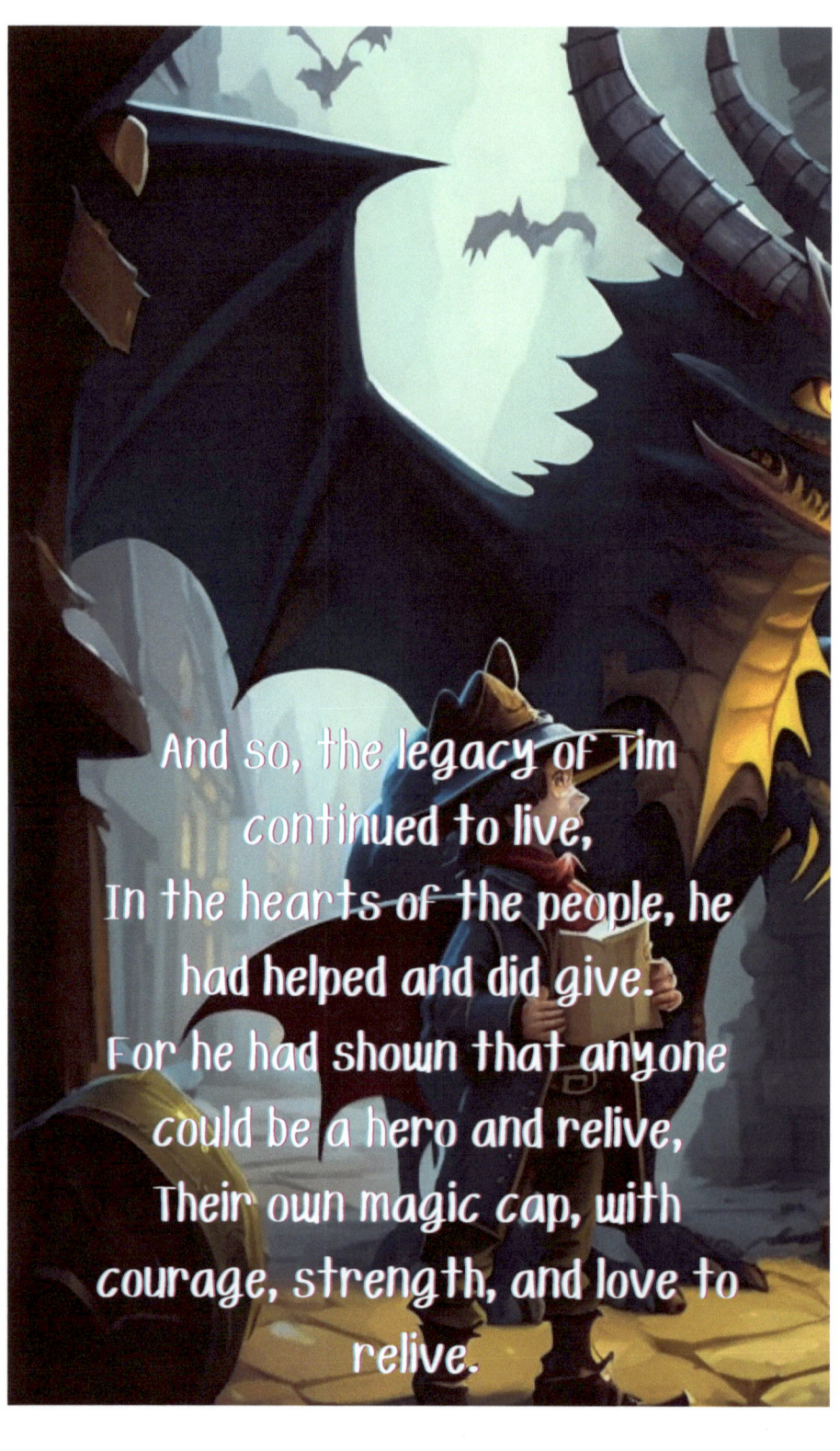

And so, the legacy of Tim continued to live,
In the hearts of the people, he had helped and did give.
For he had shown that anyone could be a hero and relive,
Their own magic cap, with courage, strength, and love to relive.